The Life, Times & Music® Series

The Life, Times & Music® Series

Timothy Frew

FRIEDMAN/FAIRFAX
PUBLISHERS

A FRIEDMAN/FAIRFAX BOOK

ISBN 1-56799-306-0

Editor: Stephen Slaybaugh
Art Director: Jeff Batzli
Designer: SMAY VISION
Photography Editor: Emilya Naymark
Production Manager: Jeanne E. Kaufman

Color separations by HK Scanner Arts International Ltd.
Printed in Hong Kong and bound in China by Midas Printing Limited

For bulk purchases and special sales, please contact:
Friedman / Fairfax Publishers
Attention: Sales Department
15 West 26th Street
New York, NY 10010
212/685-6610   FAX 212/685-1307

Website: http://www.webcom.com/friedman/

Contents

Introduction

Rockabilly is a style of rock and roll that took the country by storm in the mid-1950s. Quite literally, it is a combination of hillbilly music and rhythm and blues (R&B), as developed by such rock and roll icons as Elvis Presley, Buddy Holly, Carl Perkins, Jerry Lee Lewis, and Bill Haley, as well as lesser-known but equally as important innovators like Hardrock Gunter, Buddy Knox, Johnny and Dorsey Burnette, Billy Lee Riley, and Link Wray. It is an extremely high-energy form of music that typically relies on countrified R&B guitar, heavy slapping bass, a strong rhythm section, and lyrics about teenage angst.

There is no way of determining exactly when rock and roll started. The term was used in music as early as 1936 when the Boswell Sisters sang a song called "Rock and Roll" in a little-known movie called *Transatlantic Merry-Go-Round* and was a black euphemism for sex that had been in use well before the Boswell Sisters sang their

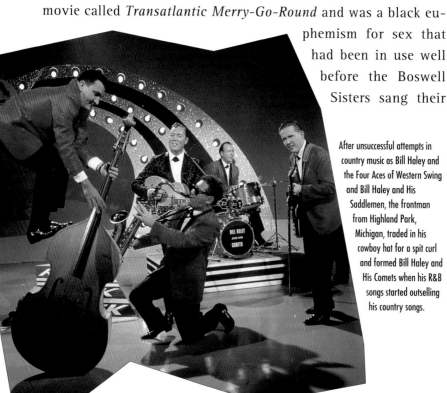

After unsuccessful attempts in country music as Bill Haley and the Four Aces of Western Swing and Bill Haley and His Saddlemen, the frontman from Highland Park, Michigan, traded in his cowboy hat for a spit curl and formed Bill Haley and His Comets when his R&B songs started outselling his country songs.

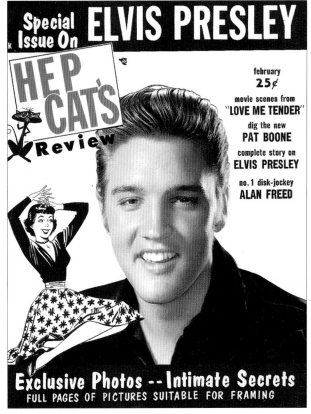

Originally billed as the "Hillbilly Cat," Elvis Presley went from being a poor truck driver to becoming the "King of Rock and Roll" in just a few short years.

song. In the 1950s, deejay Alan Freed (1922–1965) began using rock and roll to describe race-specific R&B music.

Rockabilly was the result of a bunch of young white hill-billies who were raised on country music but became drawn to the exciting sounds of black-oriented radio. Some of the earliest rockabilly recordings were country versions of existing R&B hits, or R&B versions of existing country hits. Later artists wrote their own songs that stayed true to the high-energy aspects of both musical forms.

Unlike some white artists such as Pat Boone and the Crew Cuts

Cleveland deejay Alan Freed is credited with coming up with the term "rock and roll" to describe the R&B musical revolution of the early fifties. Here he is in a still from *Mister Rock and Roll,* one of a slew of films that tried to capitalize on the rock and roll phenomenon.

who made their living by record-ing sanitized versions of black R&B songs, turning them into hits in the process, the artists of rockabilly recorded songs that were just as sexy, dangerous, and energetic as their black counter-parts. And like rhythm and blues, rockabilly developed in the small independent record companies and radio stations that were will-ing to take a chance on an excit-ing new form of music.

Paving the Path to Rock and Roll

American popular music was in a state of flux in the late forties and early fifties. The big band era, which had dominated popular music for the past twenty years, was coming to an end. The high cost of touring combined with musicians' labor disputes meant that big bands were no longer economically feasible. Bands were gradually becoming smaller, and eventually individual pop singers dominated the marketplace. Bing Crosby was the first big pop singing star to come out of the big band era, followed closely by some of the most-loved singers of all time, such as Frank Sinatra, Rosemary Clooney, Tony Bennett, Vic Damone, Dinah Shore, Jo Stafford, Perry Como, Kay Starr, and Patti Page. Competition from television caused radio to all but abandon live music broadcasts in favor of the now ubiquitous radio playlist. Network radio especially relied on playing a limited number of hit records by a few established vocalists. While the stars of the period were very talented singers and musicians, the songs they were given to sing were often little more than novelty songs. Hits such as "How Much Is That Doggie in the Window" and "If I Knew You Were Comin' I'd Have Baked a Cake" were virtually indistinguishable from the slickly produced radio jingles that were played alongside them.

Major record labels and network radio stations became extremely conservative, unwilling to take chances on new acts and new style of music. Even so, the decade following World War II saw a steep increase in the total number of record companies. Prior to 1940, there were three large

Just off Hollywood and Vine in Hollywood, California stands the "world's first circular office building" and the international home of Capitol Records, one of the large record companies that dominated the music scene in the 1950s.

The biggest singing star of the first half of the twentieth century, Bing Crosby was one of the first vocalists to take advantage of the microphone, singing into it as though he was singing to an individual listener.

companies that dominated the record business: Columbia, founded in 1889; Victor, founded in 1901; and Decca, a subsidiary of British Decca, formed in 1933. By 1950, the big three were joined by Capitol (1942), MGM (1946), and Mercury (1947). In addition to the large, big-money record companies, literally hundreds of small independent companies sprang up all over the country between 1945 and 1953, including: Atlantic, Apollo, Cadence, Ember, Jubilee, National, Rama, and Savoy in New York City; Imperial, Modern, Philo, and Specialty in Los Angeles; Savoy in Newark, New Jersey; King in Cincinnati; Bullet and Excello in Nashville; Chess and Vee-Jay in Chicago; Trumpet in Jackson, Mississippi; Dot in Houston; and Meteor and Sun in Memphis.

Alan Freed's *Rock and Roll House Party* radio show fed exciting R&B music to a hungry white audience. He also promoted a series of live rock and roll shows to sold-out audiences across the country.

It was at these small independent companies that the most innovative music was being made, and most of the changes were taking place in black R&B music. In 1949, *Billboard* magazine changed the name of its "race" chart to the R&B chart. By 1953, R&B records grossed more than fifteen million dollars—more than the entire music industry earned in 1940. By 1954, there were more than two hundred radio stations across the country catering primarily to black listeners; New York City alone had four black stations.

A Cleveland deejay named Alan Freed started playing rhythm and blues at the suggestion of a local record store owner who noticed a lot of white kids buying the records. Freed started calling the new music "rock and roll" in order to get away from the race-specific R&B label. His *Rock and Roll House Party* radio show quickly became the most popular show in town. In 1952, Freed began producing live rock and roll shows in the Cleveland area. One such dance at the Cleveland Arena billed Charles Brown, the Dominoes, the Orioles, the Moonglows, and Jimmy Forest. Seventeen thousand fans came to see the show; unfortunately, the stadium only held ten thousand and a riot ensued, almost landing Freed in jail.

The rhythm and blues/rock and roll revolution was not lost on people in the South. Dozens of hep hillbilly cats who were weaned on country, gospel, and the blues began making their own brand of music, influenced by the rhythm and blues of Chuck Berry, Arthur Crudup, Fats Domino, Little Richard, and others, as well as the country jazz and western swing of such artists as Bob Wills,

One of the earliest and most popular rock and roll stars, New Orleans singer/piano player Fats Domino was one of many black artists who influenced the "hillbilly cats" who brought rockabilly into the forefront of popular music.

the Delmore Brothers, Red Foley, and Tennessee Earnie Ford. From this musical hybrid came what was first called "cat music" and later dubbed "rockabilly."

The Early Innovators of Rockabilly

One of the earliest yet generally unrecognized originators of rockabilly music was an unlikely man by the name of Sidney "Hardrock" Gunter. Born on September 18, 1918, in the workmen's barracks of an iron mine on the outskirts of Birmingham, Alabama, Gunter began his professional musical life by playing beer joints during his time off from working the mines. His nickname actually comes not from any association with rock and roll, but from his time wielding a pickax in the mines.

Sidney "Hardrock" Gunter.

Gunter's musical style resulted directly from his upbringing in Birmingham. During the 1920s and 1930s, Birmingham was a hotbed of country music and a blues-based music known as boogie woogie. What music people listened to and played generally depended on the color of their skin. While most of white Birmingham stuck primarily to country or hillbilly music, some of the hipper whites listened to the stomping sound coming from Birmingham's black north side.

Gunter started out playing hillbilly music, but as his sound developed, he used a lot of the boogie woogie styling he heard played by black pianists such as Robert McCoy, Charles "Cow Cow" Davenport, and Pine Top Smith.

Smith, a native of Troy, Alabama, was the first musician to use the term "boogie woogie" in a song when he recorded "Pine Top's Boogie Woogie" for Brunswick (with "Pine Top's Blues" on the flip

Although he never gained the fame he deserved, Sidney "Hardrock" Gunter was a pioneer of rockabilly music. He is shown here performing on the WWVA *Jamboree* radio show in West Virginia.

Cow Cow Davenport was one of the pioneers of the Alabama Boogie Woogie that influenced the music of "Hardrock" Gunter.

side) in 1928. The song included shouted instructions for dancing boogie woogie. While Smith enjoyed only marginal success with the song, Tommy Dorsey scored a hit when he recorded the song, retitled "Boogie Woogie," in 1938 with the Clark Sisters singing vocals. Since then, scores of other artists have recorded it. Unfortunately, Smith didn't live long enough to enjoy his legacy: less then a year after recording "Pine Top's Boogie Woogie," he was killed by a stray bullet during a barroom shoot-out at Odd Fellows Hall in Chicago.

By 1939, the twenty-one-year-old Gunter had grown tired of the hard life of the iron mines, and he took a job as a singing deejay at Birmingham's largest radio station: WAPI–"The Voice of Alabama." Keeping his nickname, he performed on the radio both as a solo act and as part of Happy Wilson's Golden River Boys. A few years later, Hardrock formed Hardrock and the Pebbles, a six-piece country boogie band that included a fiddler, a pedal-steel guitar player, a bass player, a drummer, and a boogie woogie piano player.

In 1950, Hardrock signed with local Bama Records and recorded "Birmingham Bounce," a Gunter original, which used the word "rockin'" several times throughout the song. By May 1950, "Birmingham Bounce" had knocked Hank Williams' "Long Gone Lonesome Blues" out of the number one slot on the country music charts.

Hardrock followed up his initial success with "Gonna Dance All Night" and "Lonesome Blues," both released in July 1950. While neither song sold particularly well, "Gonna Dance All Night" features a driving backbeat and a chorus in which Hardrock repeatedly yells, "We're gonna rock and roll!"

In 1951, Hardrock signed with Decca and recorded "Boogie Woogie on a Saturday Night," "I've Done Gone Hog Wild," and "Sixty-Minute Man." Although the term "boogie woogie" had not yet been coined, "Boogie Woogie on a Saturday Night" and "I've Done Gone Hog Wild" are clearly rockabilly records that had the same energy and were of the same country and R&B hybrid which would later make such artists as Elvis Presley and Carl Perkins famous. Gunter's "Sixty-Minute Man" is a strange country version of the Dominoes' R&B hit about a man who could have sex for sixty minutes straight.

Once again, Gunter's recordings were more groundbreaking than they were sellable, and the rockabilly pioneer was eventually dropped by Decca. After a brief stint in the army, Hardrock returned to music as a member of WWVA's Jamboree in Wheeling, West Virginia, and in 1954 he found his way to Sam Phillips's Sun Records in Memphis. There he recorded a new, rocking version of Gonna Dance All Night," but once again the song failed to sell. A few months later Sun released the first record by the most famous rockabilly artist of all time—Elvis Presley—and Hardrock was quickly forgotten.

Equally obscure but no less groundbreaking was a club owner and rockabilly piano player named Roy Hall. Born in a small Appalachian town in Virginia, Hall learned piano as a teenager from an old black local. By the time he was twenty-one, Hall had started traveling the bar circuit in Virginia, Tennessee, and Alabama, playing

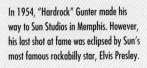

In 1954, "Hardrock" Gunter made his way to Sun Studios in Memphis. However, his last shot at fame was eclipsed by Sun's most famous rockabilly star, Elvis Presley.

Wanda Jackson (b. 1937)

Wanda Jackson was one of the first and few female rockabillies of the 1950s. She switched from country to rock and roll after sharing a bill with Elvis Presley on the *Hank Snow Jamboree*.

When you think of a rockabilly singer, what comes to mind is a wild-eyed country boy with hair piled high, shirt sleeves rolled up, and an electric guitar slung low. While it is true that rockabilly music was primarily dominated by men during the late 1950s, there was one female performer who broke through the ranks to score several top forty hits and to gain worldwide fame.

Wanda Lavonne Jackson was born to a poor Oklahoma farming family, but like thousands of other Okies, her family moved west, to Bakersfield, California, after a six-year drought destroyed nearly 200,000 square miles (516,000 sq km) of Oklahoma topsoil. By the late 1940s, Bakersfield, with its Blackboard Dance Hall, was already becoming a hotbed of country music. The first to gain fame there was Jean Shephard, the "Queen of Honky-Tonk Music." Later Bakersfield stars included Tommy Collins, Buck Owens, and Merle Haggard.

It was in this music-rich environment that Jackson's father taught her how to play the guitar and piano and instilled in her a great love of country music. Before long, however, the family packed up their possessions once more and headed back to Oklahoma, where Jackson had her own radio show at the tender age of thirteen. After graduating from high school, she joined Hank Thompson and the Brazos Valley Boys.

By 1954, when Jackson joined the band, Hank Thompson had already established himself as one of the most famous exponents of western swing, a form of country music pioneered by fiddler and bandleader Bob Wills. Thompson's early top five hits included "Waiting in the Lobby of Your Heart" (1952), "Wild Side of Life" (1952), "Rub-A-Dub-Dub" (1953), and "Wake Up Irene" (1953). Taken by Jackson's strong country voice, Thompson recorded a duet with her for Decca, "You Can't Have My Love," which reached number eight on *Billboard*'s country and western chart in 1954. Due to the success of that song, Thompson invited her to join him on the "Hank Snow Jamboree," a bill that featured a young phenom named Elvis Presley.

It was after seeing Elvis perform that Jackson decided she wanted to be a rockabilly singer. Decca, who had signed her as a country singer, and Hank Thompson wanted no part of rock and roll, so she switched to Capitol in 1956 to become one of the few female rockers of the fifties.

Her first hit was "Let's Have a Party," which cracked the pop top forty in both the United States and the United Kingdom. She followed that

Wanda Jackson with Billy Gray, her duet partner in Hank Thompson and the Brazos Valley Boys. "You Can't Have My Love" reached number eight on *Billboard's* country and western chart in 1954.

with "Mean, Mean Man," "Right Or Wrong," and "In the Middle of a Heartache," all top-forty hits in 1961. Although she never gained superstardom as a rockabilly singer in the States, she was quite popular in Holland, Germany, and Japan, where she cut alternate versions of her hits in these languages such as her infamous "Fujiyama Mama."

As rockabilly faded in the early sixties, Jackson switched to female honky-tonk music, forming a band called the Party Timers with her husband, Wendell Goodman. Between 1961 and 1971, she racked up twenty-five country hits, including "A Girl Don't Have to Drink to Have Fun" and "Tears Will Be a Chaser for Your Heart."

Roy Hall is shown here in a photo taken for the cover of his album *Boogie Rockabilly*.

and singing for free drinks and loose change. His piano style was boogie woogie and rhythm and blues, but his vocal style was pure hillbilly.

In the mid-1940s, Hall formed Roy Hall and the Cohutta Mountain Boys, who were signed by Fortune Records in Detroit in 1949. Fortune released six songs by Hall, none of which sold particularly well. Leaving his band up north, Hall moved to Nashville, and after a few minor releases on Bullet he opened a nightclub, where he hired such talent as the still-unknown Elvis Presley and Jerry Lee Lewis.

In 1954, Hall and a black musician named Dave Williams went on a hunting trip that provided inspiration for one of the most famous rockabilly songs of all time, "Whole Lotta Shakin' Goin' On." In *Unsung Heroes of Rock 'n' Roll,* author Nick Tosches quotes Hall: "We was down in Pahokee, on Lake Okeechobee. We was down there, out on a damn pond, fishin' an' milkin' snakes. Drinkin' wine mostly. There was a bunch of us down there....See, this guy down there had a big bell that he'd ring to git us all to come in to dinner; an' I call over there to th' other part of the island, I say, 'What's goin' on?' Colored guy said, 'We got twenty-one drums'—see, we was all drunk—'we got an ol' bass horn an' they even keepin' time on a ding-dong.' See, that was the big bell they'd ring to git us t'come in."

From this came these lyrics:

Twenty-one drums and an ol' bass horn,
Somebody beatin' on a ding-dong.
Come on over, baby,
whole lotta shakin' goin' on.

Hall recorded "Whole Lotta Shakin' Goin' On" for Decca in 1955 and continued to cut rockabilly records for them through 1956, but none of his records were ever hits. One year later, Jerry Lee Lewis sent "Whole Lotta Shakin' Goin' On" to number one on the country and R&B charts and to number three on the pop charts.

While there were many artists who played a combination of country boogie, hillbilly, and rhythm and blues prior to 1953, it took an unassuming, struggling twenty-eight-year-old country singer from the north to put rockabilly music on the top of the pop charts.

Born in Highland Park, Michigan, Bill Haley (1925–1981) moved to suburban Philadelphia with his family when he was seven years old. As a young teenager, Haley built his own guitar and taught himself how to play it. A lover of country music, Haley got his first

After several attempts at country music, "Yodeling" Bill Haley finally gained stardom after switching to rock and roll. Unlike most of the other rockabilly legends, Haley was a northerner, born in Michigan and raised in Pennsylvania.

paying gig at the age of thirteen, playing and singing at an auction house for a dollar a night. He lived in Connecticut briefly in 1944, where he joined a country band, the Down-homers, who recorded "We're Recruiting" and "Out Where the West Winds Blow." Later that year, he left the band and got a job as a deejay at WSNJ in Bridgeport, New Jersey (a Philadelphia suburb), where he became known as Yodeling Bill Haley.

In 1948, Haley took a job at WPWA in Chester, Pennsylvania, where he remained as musical director until 1954. It was there that Haley also formed his first

Bill Haley and His Comets' cultivated "hep cat" image and elaborately staged live shows helped them become one of the most popular rockabilly acts of the early fifties. While Haley had fourteen top forty hits between 1953 and 1958, he never came close to duplicating the success he enjoyed with "Rock Around the Clock," the best selling single of all time.

band, Bill Haley and the Four Aces of Western Swing. The band signed with a tiny local label named Cowboy Records and recorded covers of recent country hits like George Morgan's "Candy Kisses," Red Foley's "Tennessee Border," and Hank Williams' "Too Many Parties, Too Many Pals." In 1949, after changing its name to Bill Haley and the Saddlemen, the band got its first national release: "Why Do I Cry Over You" and "I'm Gonna Dry Every Tear with a Kiss," two songs originally recorded for Keystone Records, but leased to Atlantic. Neither song made the country charts.

In 1950, Haley signed with Dave Miller's Holiday Records (whose biggest star was mood music conductor Monty Kelly) and recorded his first noncountry songs—cover versions of the R&B hits "Rocket 88" (Jackie Brenston) and "Rock the Joint" (Jimmy Preston). After releasing "Jukebox Cannonball," which set hipster lyrics to Roy Acuff's country hit "Wabash Cannonball," Haley realized that his R&B songs were selling much better then his country songs, so he

Haley's biggest break came when "Rock Around the Clock" was featured in the hit movie *Blackboard Jungle*. The film's music director was Jimmy Myers, a.k.a. Jimmy DeKnight, one of the authors of the song.

hung up his cowboy hat and suit, donned a dinner jacket and baggy pants, gave himself a spit curl, and changed the name of the band to Bill Haley and the Comets.

The band hit pay dirt with its second release: "Crazy Man, Crazy" came out on Essex Records (formerly Holiday) in 1953 and soon rose to number fifteen on the pop charts. It was the first rock and roll or R&B song by a white artist to hit the pop charts, giving

white mainstream America its first taste of what had been playing for years on the small R&B and country radio stations
across the country.

The success of "Crazy, Man, Crazy" took Haley to Decca, where
he hooked up with Milt Gabler, who had produced many of Joe
Turner's jump blues hits of the 1940s. The first song Haley recorded
at Decca was "Rock Around the Clock" by Max Freedman, the Tin
Pan Alley author of "Sioux City Sue" and "Blue Danube Waltz,"
and Jimmy DeKnight, the pen name of Jimmy Myers of Myers
Music, who also published the song.

The song was little more than a novelty tune, but Gabler
recorded the band in an empty ballroom with a high ceiling, which
allowed them to play loud and gave the song its energetic rockabilly feel. When it was first released, "Rock Around the Clock" was
a commercial failure despite a relatively strong marketing push
from Decca that included a full-page ad in *Billboard* magazine.
The next Haley release was a cover of the Big Joe Turner R&B hit
"Shake, Rattle, and Roll," which rose to number ten in 1954.

Haley's biggest break came when the Glen Ford/Sidney Poitier
film *Blackboard Jungle* was released in 1955. The music director
for the film was none other than Jimmy Myers, a.k.a. Jimmy
DeKnight, coauthor of "Rock Around the Clock." Haley's original
recording was featured predominantly in the movie soundtrack.
The song shot to number one on the pop charts two years after its
original release and went on to become the best-selling single of
all time, with more than twenty-five million copies sold.

Bill Haley was an extremely unlikely rock and roll hero. Despite
his forced hepcat image, he was very clean-cut and well mani-
cured. He was slightly overweight, had a weak voice, and, at thirty
years old, was much older and tamer then the young, wild masters
of rockabilly that were about to follow him onto the pop charts.

Haley had fourteen top-forty hits between 1953 and 1958, but
never another number one after "Rock Around the Clock." His next-
highest appearance on the charts was for "See You Later, Alligator,"
which hit number six in 1956. Haley simply lacked the charisma,
sex appeal, and danger to become a true rockabilly madman.

Sun Records and the Rockabilly Triumvirate

Much of the early history of rockabilly—and rock and roll in general—was centered around a small recording studio and record company located at 706 Union Avenue in Memphis, Tennessee. A former deejay named Sam Phillips (b. 1923) started the Memphis Recording Studio, a small business with the motto "We Record Anything—Anywhere—Anytime." "Anything" included weddings, birthday parties, public speeches, and anyone willing to come in and pay four dollars to sing a song. The recordings were made directly onto acetate discs, which the singer could take home as soon as the taping was finished.

Sam Phillips' Memphis Recording Studio, the home of Sun Records, is where many of the initial rockabilly recordings were made.

Sensing a need for a local label that catered to black musicians, Phillips acquired the talent of local deejay Dewey Phillips (no relation). The original idea was to record local talent and to press and distribute their own records. However, all the early Phillips masters were leased to independent labels such as Chess, Modern, Meteor, RPM, and Trumpet. Still, such notable jazz, blues, and R&B talent as Phineas Newborn, B.B. King, Howlin' Wolf (Chester Burnett), Walter Horton, Earl Hooker, Bobby Bland, and Joe

"Bear Cat," written by Sam Phillips and recorded by Rufus Thomas, Jr., was the first hit on Sun Records. The song was a comic send-up of Big Mama Thorton's "Hound Dog." Phillips was successfully sued for copyright infringement on the song.

Hill Louis recorded at Phillips' studio. One of the earliest Phillips recordings was the seminal R&B hit "Rocket 88" by Jackie Brenston and his Delta Cats, who were actually Ike Turner's Kings of Rhythm (Jackie Brenston was Ike's saxophone player). Many people consider "Rocket 88," which was covered by Bill Haley and other artists, to be the first true rock and roll song. While Phillips' studio was able to stay afloat, it was still not the self-sustaining record company that its owner had envisioned.

One Sun act, Doug Poindexter and the Starlight Wranglers, included bassist Bill Black (far left) and guitarist Scotty Moore (far right). The duo would eventually team up with Elvis Presley.

In 1952, Phillips decided to take another stab at launching his own label, and Sun Records was born. The first hit on Sun was Rufus Thomas, Jr.'s "Bear Cat," a comic answer to the Big Mama Thornton hit "Hound Dog." Phillips followed this success with R&B hits by Junior Parker and his Blue Flames and Billy "The Kid" Emerson.

When he first interviewed Elvis Presley on the radio, Dewey Phillips asked the King what high school he went to in order to let the listeners know that Presley was white.

While Sun's bread and butter was with black blues and R&B musicians, the label also dabbled in country music with such bands as the Ripley Cotton Choppers, Earl Peterson, Malcolm Yelvington and the Star Rhythm Boys, and Doug Poindexter and the Starlight Wranglers. Phillips always said that if he could find a white boy that could sing like a black man, he could make a million dollars. Perhaps that's what originally drew him to Hardrock Gunter. While Hardrock did not sing like a black man, his music was certainly influenced by black rhythm and blues and boogie woogie. Unfortunately, Hardrock was too old by the time he made it to Sun and was not the vibrant, wild rockabilly that Phillips was looking for. Phillips found that man the day Elvis Aron Presley (1935–1977) walked into his studio.

In late August 1953, Elvis Presley, guitar in hand, walked into the Memphis Recording Studio (Phillips still ran this profitable sideline) to record two songs for his mother's birthday. Phillips' assistant, Marion Keisker, was running the booth that day. Halfway through Elvis' first song, the early Ink Spots hit "My Happiness,"

With his country-boy attitude, dangerous good looks, and slicked-back hair, Elvis Presley was the ultimate rockabilly performer. He took the country and gospel of his musical heritage and infused them with a heavy dose of rhythm and blues to introduce an entirely new sound to the country.

Brenda Lee (b. 1944)

Brenda Lee possessed a strong, vibrant voice that was equally at home in rockabilly and country music.

Brenda Lee was one of the most prolific and successful crossover singers of the 1960s. Her big voice and characteristic use of melisma were well suited to both country music and rock and roll.

A child singing prodigy, Lee began her professional career in 1949 singing on the radio in Congers, Georgia, at the age of five. She signed with Decca in 1955 when she was only eleven years old, and had minor country hits that year with "One Step at a Time" and "Dynamite." Between 1955 and 1959, she took her act to television, appearing on such shows as Red Foley's *Jubilee USA*, *The Steve Allen Show*, *The Perry Como Show*, and, in the United Kingdom, Jack Good's *Oh Boy*.

It wasn't until Lee took advantage of her strong, vibrant voice and started to sing more rockabilly-style songs that she gained radio popularity. In 1959 and 1960, Lee's country stardom faded, but she scored big on both the R&B and pop charts with "Sweet Nothin's," "I'm Sorry," "That's All You Gotta Do," and "I Want to Be Wanted," all number one pop hits and top-twenty R&B hits. As one of the few female rockabilly performers, Lee became known as "Little Miss Dynamite."

By 1964, the rockabilly era had pretty much given way to the British invasion and American folk rock. Lee married Ronnie Shacklett, her childhood sweetheart; settled in Nashville; had two daughters, Julie and Jolie; and went back to country music. Lee never had another number one pop hit, but she was a regular fixture on the country charts throughout the 1970s and 1980s.

Keisker noticed something unique about Presley's voice and started a tape machine to make a backup copy to play for Phillips.

Keisker later stated, "The reason I taped Elvis was this. Over and over I remember Sam saying, 'If I could find a white man who had the Negro sound and the Negro feel, I could make a million dollars.' This is what I heard in Elvis...what they now call soul."

On the flip side of the acetate, Elvis recorded another Ink Spots song, "That's When the Heartache Begins." Elvis later described the recording as sounding like "somebody pounding on a bucket."

Phillips apparently heard something in the recordings and put Elvis in touch with Scotty Moore, a young guitarist who played with Doug Poindexter and the Starlight Wranglers, and bassist Bill Black. Phillips thought that Moore, with his hard-edged electric guitar sound and flowery, exuberant playing style, would be a natural complement to young Presley's voice. Moore and Phillips had also had many lengthy conversations about developing a new musical

Sam Phillips was the recording innovator that helped Presley develop his exciting new sound. The early Sun recordings used no drums—only two guitars, a bass, and Presley's voice to capture the distinctive rockabilly feel.

While his records gradually gained in popularity, it was through his live performances that Elvis achieved early notoriety. Here, Elvis, Scotty, and Bill perform at Messick High School in 1955.

style—one that would combine country, blues, gospel, and pop elements of both white and black music.

On July 5, 1954, Presley, Moore, and Black went into Sun for their first recording session. After several hours and many failed songs, Phillips told the band to take a break. Just for fun, Elvis started playing an upbeat version of the "Big Boy" Crudup blues standard "That's All Right (Mama)" while dancing and bopping

around the studio as he slapped his acoustic guitar and sang. Moore and Black quickly joined in on the fun, and pretty soon the three of them began rocking around the studio. Listening from the control room, Phillips knew he had found his new sound.

Popular Memphis deejay Dewey Phillips helped introduce black R&B music to white Memphis teenagers. He was also the first person to play an Elvis Presley record on the air.

The newly inspired band finished their first single that day, with "That's All Right (Mama)" on the A side and a rocking version of Bill Monroe's bluegrass classic "Blue Moon of Kentucky" on the B side. Two days later, Sam delivered an acetate disc of the record to Dewey Phillips for his WHBQ R&B radio show, "Red Hot and Blue," and Elvis got his first radio play. Dewey was so enraptured by the fresh sound that he played the two songs over and over again. Pretty soon the switchboard at the radio station was lighting up and Elvismania had begun. A few days after the broadcast, orders for seven thousand copies of the record came in—and Sam Phillips had not even pressed the master disc yet.

On July 19, 1954, "That's All Right (Mama)"/"Blue Moon of Kentucky" (Sun 209) was officially released. The record quickly became a hit in Memphis, climbing to number three on the local chart and selling more than twenty thousand copies. Nationally, however, it got minimal attention. Few deejays were willing to play the record: it was too hillbilly for some and too black for the rest.

Billed as the Hillbilly Cat and the Blue Moon Boys, Presley, Moore, and Black played their first live performance on an all-country music bill at the Overton Park Shell in Memphis, with Webb Pierce and headliner Slim Whitman. Elvis performed "That's

The Million Dollar Quartet

From left to right: Jerry Lee Lewis, Carl Perkins, Elvis Presley, and Johnny Cash, otherwise known as the Million Dolllar Quartet. Tapes of the now imfamous jam session at Sun Studios were not released to the public until the 1980s.

On December 4, 1956, Carl Perkins was at Sun Records recording "Matchbox" and "True to Your Love." Less then a year earlier, Perkins had hit the jackpot with his smash "Blue Suede Shoes," the song that knocked "Heartbreak Hotel," by former Sun star Elvis Presley, from the number one spot on the charts. Backing Perkins were his two brothers, J.B. on rhythm guitar and Clayton on bass, and Fluke Holland on drums. Producer Jack Clement had also asked Jerry Lee Lewis, whose first Sun record, "Crazy Arms"/"End of the Road," had been released three days earlier, to sit in on piano. Perkins had invited his friend Johnny Cash (who had already scored a cross-over hit with "I Walk the Line") to stop by and watch.

Toward the end of the session, Elvis Presley came in with Marilyn Evans, a dancer he had met during his recent engagement in Las Vegas. A few years earlier, before either one had made it big, Presley and Perkins toured the South together, playing beer halls, fairs, and honky tonks. On this day, however, Presley was the biggest singing star in the country, with over twenty-seven million records sold in his first year with RCA. Perkins, on the other hand, was trying to regain the success he had with "Blue Suede Shoes."

Presley sat down at the piano to play and sing a few bars of the Fats Domino hit "Blueberry Hill," and was quickly joined by Perkins, Lewis, and Cash. Jack Clement, sensing something amazing was about to happen, put a fresh tape in the machine and began to record.

According to Sun session guitarist Charles Underwood, "I (didn't) think there was going to be a jam session, but then I mentioned that I had an acoustic guitar in the trunk of my car....There's something about an acoustic guitar that lends itself to jam sessions...."

And jam they did, for almost three hours. The musicians ran through parts of more than forty songs, running the gamut from gospel to hillbilly to rhythm and blues. In one short afternoon, the three rockabilly superstars (Johnny Cash left soon after the jam session began) laughed, sang, and jammed their way through practically all of the musical genres that came together to make rockabilly music.

Sensing an opportunity for good publicity, Sam Phillips called Robert Johnson of the Memphis Press-Scimitar, who came by with staff photographer George Pierce. The next day Johnson wrote:

> "I never had a better time than yesterday when I dropped in at Sam Phillips' Sun Record bedlam.... It was what one might call a barrelhouse of fun. Carl Perkins was in a recording session....Johnny Cash dropped by. Jerry Lee Lewis was there, too, and then Elvis stopped by....The joint was really rocking before they got thru....If Sam Phillips had been on his toes, he'd have turned on the recorder....That quartet could sell a million."

The "recorder" had been turned on, but the tapes from the soon to be infamous "Million Dollar Quartet" would not be heard by the public until twenty-four years later—three years after Elvis Presley's death. The first release of the tapes was in 1980 on a bootleg called *The Million Dollar Quartet*, which included only seventeen songs from the session. Seven years later, another bootleg, *The One Million Dollar Quartet*, was released, containing the seventeen songs from the original bootleg plus twenty-two more tracks.

The recordings of the session were not officially released until BMG, RCA, and Sun released *Elvis Presley: The Million Dollar Quartet* in 1990. Containing forty-one tracks in all, this inspiring if primitive album documents the energy, spontaneity, and influences of rockabilly music better than any other single recording.

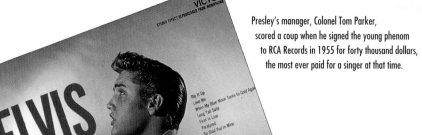

All Right (Mama)" and a cover of the Wynonie Harris R&B hit "Good Rockin' Tonight." Presley worked up the crowd so much with his brief set that Pierce, who was scheduled to go on after Elvis, refused to perform.

In a later interview, Elvis recalled, "Everybody was screaming and everything, and I came offstage and my manager told me that they was hollering because I was wiggling. And so I went back out for an encore, and I did a little more. And the more I did, the wilder they went."

Elvis helped defined the term "rockabilly." He was young, sexy, exciting, and dangerous, and he belted out his songs as if the world were coming to an end. While his Sun recordings were truly groundbreaking in their mixture of hillbilly music and rhythm and blues, it was in his live performances that the real Presley exuberance came out.

Elvis and the band built up their reputation with a nonstop touring schedule that took them to bars, honky-tonks, country music nightclubs, and fairs (sometimes playing on the back of a flatbed truck) across the South. Traveling from Florida to New Mexico, the band played at practically any venue that would hire them. With each performance, the Presley following grew. With his greased hair, black-and-pink suits, curled lip, and gyrating hips, Elvis exuded a sexual aura that at once attracted and served as a release for the repressed youth of the 1950s. Elvis did onstage what was considered improper for young people to even think about, and the young people (especially women) went crazy over him. Unlike the much milder Bill Haley, Elvis was the consummate rockabilly wild man.

In Presley's subsequent Sun recordings, Phillips was careful to keep the rockabilly mixture of country and rhythm and blues alive, going as far as releasing singles with a rocked up R&B song on the A side and a country-oriented B side. His next two singles were "Good Rockin' Tonight"/"I Don't Care If the Sun Don't Shine" and "Milkcow Blues Boogie"/"You're a Heartbreaker," neither of which sold very well. However, his third Sun release, "Baby Let's Play House"/"I'm Left, You're Right, She's Gone," reached number ten on *Billboard* magazine's country chart. He followed that success with "Mystery Train"/"I Forgot to Remember to Forget," which reached number eleven on the country charts in August 1955. That same month *Billboard* named him the eighth most promising country and western vocalist, and stated that he was "the hottest piece of merchandise on the Louisiana Hayride." Deejays across the country were suddenly playing Presley records with a determined

Elvis earned a reputation early on for performances that electrified kids and offended adults.

Colonel Tom Parker (third from left) negotiated a deal for Elvis with RCA records, which Sun Records president Sam Phillips also benefitted from.

regularity. A new youth music movement was sweeping the country. In Cleveland, deejay Alan Freed dubbed the new music rock and roll, and Elvis was quickly establishing himself as the movement's forerunner.

One person who saw great potential in Elvis was Colonel Tom Parker (b. 1909), a former carny barker–turned–country music manager whose real name was Andreas Cornelius van Kuijk. Parker, who had previously managed country singers Eddie Arnold and Hank Snow, saw a great deal of talent and moneymaking possibilities in Elvis, and on August 15, 1955, managed to lure Presley away from his current manager, Bob Neal. The contract that Elvis signed with Parker gave the manager twenty-five percent of everything Elvis made.

Parker's first order of business was to get Presley signed to a major label. Sam Phillips knew that with Colonel Parker in the picture, Elvis' days at Sun were numbered, but Phillips was not completely adverse to losing Elvis. Presley was on the verge of becoming a mammoth singing sensation. Parker had begun negotiating a major national tour for Presley, as well as possible television appearances, and Phillips knew that if Elvis were to have a really big national hit, it could virtually destroy a small company like Sun Records. Phillips simply did not have the capital necessary to press and distribute a million-selling record. Besides, if Parker could arrange a lucrative deal with a major label, Sun Records would receive enough capital for Phillips to push his latest young prodigy, rockabilly singer/guitarist Carl Perkins (b. 1932).

On November 20, 1955, Presley, Parker, and Phillips finalized an agreement with RCA. The forty thousand dollars paid by RCA was the most ever paid for the recording rights to a singer at that time. As part of the agreement, Phillips received fifteen thousand dollars for the rights to Elvis' Sun recordings.

Colonel Parker once told Presley: "You stay talented and sexy, and I'll make us both rich as rajahs." While Phillips never became as rich as a rajah off Elvis, Phillips' days as a purveyor of rockabilly were far from over.

Carl Lee Perkins, the second of three brothers, was born on a welfare-supported tenant farm near Tiptonville, Tennessee. He spent his early years living and working on a planta-tion in Lake County, where the members of his family were the only white share-croppers. In 1945, Perkins moved to Bemis, working there as a laborer in a bat-tery plant and also in nearby Jackson in a bakery.

Like Elvis, Perkins grew up listening to blues, country, and gospel music. He learned to play the guitar at an early age and won a talent con-

An excellent guitar player and accomplished songwriter, Carl Perkins' rockabilly anthem "Blue Suede Shoes" knocked Elvis' first RCA release, "Heartbreak Hotel," from the number one spot in 1956.

test at the age of thirteen, playing and singing a song that he wrote called "Movie Magg." He taught his brothers Jay and Clayton how to play the guitar, and in 1947, the three of them formed the Perkins Brothers Band. They played at a local honky-tonk called the El Rancho Club, as well as on WDXT radio in Jackson.

By 1954, Carl had made a demo tape that he

sent out to dozens of record companies in Nashville and New York; no one contacted him. It was while he and his wife, Valda Crider, were living in a subsidized housing project in Jackson that Carl heard Elvis singing "Blue Moon of Kentucky" on the radio. Perkins was so taken by the raw energy of the song that he went to Memphis with his brothers and camped out on the doorstep of Sun Studios.

Phillips gave Perkins an audition and quickly signed him to Flip Records, a subsidiary of Sun. In early 1955, Flip released the two country songs "Movie Magg" and "Turn Around," both Perkins originals. Perkins followed these with two rockabilly originals called "Juke Box Keep Playing" and "Gone, Gone, Gone." The songs got good response on local radio stations, so Phillips signed Perkins to the Sun label.

In 1956, one month after Elvis left for RCA, Perkins scored his first big hit with "Blue Suede Shoes," a song inspired by a remark he overheard at a dance. "Blue Suede Shoes" was the original rockabilly anthem. It tells the story of a poor young hillbilly who has nothing to look forward to

Knowing that he did not have the resources to support a star of the magnitude of Elvis Presley, Sam Phillips sold his recording rights to RCA and used the money to promote his latest rockabilly star, Carl Perkins.

The Killer's first number one hit was a cover of the Roy Hall rockabilly classic "Whole Lotta Shakin' Goin' On." Lewis worked in Hall's nightclub before he went to record at Sun Records

except a life of hard work. His only enjoyment and pride comes from getting duded up on Saturday night, putting on his blue suede shoes and going to the dance.

"Blue Suede Shoes" went straight to the top of *Billboard*'s pop and country charts, knocking Elvis' first RCA release, "Heartbreak Hotel," from the number one spot.

Perkins followed this success with "Boppin' the Blues," "Your True Love," and "Dixie Fried," all of which were top ten country hits and minor pop hits. It seemed that, like Presley, Perkins was about to break out into the big time. Unlike Presley, Perkins was an excellent songwriter, the consummate rock and roll guitar player, and a performer with a true rockabilly heart. Whereas Presley was more pure rock and roll and began to venture off into ballads, Perkins stayed closer to the rockabilly flavor of a Saturday night country rave-up.

Perkins was on his way to New York to appear on Ed Sullivan's and Perry Como's television shows (and to possible national stardom) when he was in a car accident that sidelined him for several months. Elvis, in the meantime, covered "Blue Suede Shoes," and Perkins' career was never the same.

Perkins signed with Columbia Records in 1958 and had minor hits with "Pink Pedal Pushers" and "Pointed Toe Shoes," continuing in the "shoe" genre he started with "Blue Suede Shoes." In the 1960s, he abandoned rockabilly for pure country music, but he proved to

be one of the biggest rockabilly influences, both in his guitar playing
and his songwriting.

While Perkins' rock and roll
career stalled in the late fifties, the
third member of the Sun Records rockabilly triumvirate went on to pose a serious threat to Presley's self-proclaimed
title as the "King of Rock and Roll." Jerry
Lee Lewis (b. 1935), nicknamed "the Killer" in school, had a classic
rockabilly vocal style and a manic, key-pounding piano style.

Lewis made an audition tape for Sun producer Jack Clement
in late 1956. Sam Phillips liked the sound of the young hillbilly
from Ferriday, Louisiana, and signed him to Sun. Lewis' first single
was a cover of a Ray Price country tune called "Crazy Arms" backed
by a Jerry Lee original called "End of the Road."

Like Elvis, Jerry Lee Lewis did not pursue the writing aspect
of music, but instead relied on material that Phillips found for him.
In his entire career, Lewis has been credited with writing only five

Like Elvis Presley and Carl Perkins before him, Jerry Lee Lewis developed under the tutelage of Sun Records
President Sam Phillips.

Possessing a classic rockabilly voice and hepped-up hillbilly looks, Jerry Lee Lewis used his frenetic live show to gain a reputation as a true rockabilly madman. His career, however, never fully recovered from the scandal of his marriage to his thirteen-year-old cousin.

songs: "End of the Road," High School Confidential," "Lewis Boogie," Lincoln Limousine," and "He Took It Like a Man."

In order to season Jerry Lee as a performer, Phillips sent him on tour with two other Sun acts, Carl Perkins and Johnny Cash. Perkins said that after the first few shows, because Jerry Lee was acting too shy, Perkins told him to "make a fuss. So the next night he carried on, stood up, [and] kicked the stool back, and a new Jerry Lee was born."

Lewis' next release was "Whole Lotta Shakin' Goin' On," which, in 1957, hit number one on the country and R&B charts and number three on the pop chart, making it the biggest hit in Sun Records' history. This success was quickly followed by "Great Balls of Fire" (written by Otis Blackwell, the author of the Presley hits "Don't Be Cruel" and "All Shook Up"), "Breathless," and "High School Confidential"—all three of which were huge hits on *Billboard*'s country, R&B, and pop charts.

Lewis was the most flamboyant, exciting, feared, and despised rockabilly performer of the fifties. Elvis was sexy and wild on stage, but at heart he was just a mama's boy. Perkins was a guitar virtuoso and rockabilly innovator, but his lifestyle was relatively tame. Even rockabilly wild men such as Eddie Cochran and Gene Vincent could not hold a candle to the unpredictable antics of Jerry Lee Lewis. He was like nothing white America had ever seen, and perhaps the only black performer that could outdo him in outrageousness was another piano pounder, Little Richard.

While touring with an Alan Freed–produced show, Lewis was angry that he had to open for Chuck Berry. When he finished his songs, Lewis set his piano on fire and stormed offstage screaming: "I'd like to see any son of bitch follow that!"

Just as Lewis was about to begin a twenty-seven-date European tour, news broke that he had married his thirteen-year-old cousin Myra without having officially divorced his second wife. The sensationalist U.K. press had a heyday with the story; as a result, Jerry Lee was booed off the stage, and his tour was canceled after three shows.

Lewis didn't help matters much with his explanation to the British press: "Myra and I are legally married. It was my second marriage that wasn't legal. I was a bigamist when I was sixteen. I was fourteen when I was first married. That lasted a year, then I met June. One day she said she was goin' to have my baby. I was real worried. Her father threatened me, and her brothers were hunting me with hide whips. So I married her just a week before my divorce from Dorothy. It was a shotgun wedding." Lewis' career was stalled by the scandal. His only top-forty hit through the seventies was "What'd I Say," which reached number thirty in 1961.

Jerry Lee Lewis was the last of the famous rockabilly legends to come out of Sun Records, although Sun was the home of many other fine rockabilly singers and songwriters, such as Billy Lee Riley, Doug Poindexter, Malcolm Yelvington, Warren Smith, Charlie Feathers, and others, as well as country stars like Johnny Cash and Charlie Pride. Roy Orbison (1936–1988) also recorded a few songs for Sun, including "Ooby Dooby," but he would go on to greater rockabilly fame with Monument Records. Orbison, however, got his start in a little studio in Clovis, New Mexico, owned by Norman Petty.

Sleepy LaBeef (b. 1935)

Although he's been playing and recording since the rockabilly heyday, Sleepy LaBeef has never gained national recognition. Today, he still performs to sold-out audiences at small venues.

Like other rockabilly aficionados, Thomas Paulsley "Sleepy" LaBeef was from a poor southern family, sang in the church, was raised on hillbilly music, and rocked to the sounds of the black rhythm and blues he heard on the radio. Unlike other successful rockabilly performers, however, LaBeef gained very little notoriety until well after the rockabilly craze was over.

The youngest of ten children in an Arkansas farming family (the original family name was LaBoeuf, the family changed it to LaBeff, and Sleepy changed it to LaBeef),

Thomas got his nickname at school because of a droopy eyelid. At the age of fourteen, he traded his rifle in for a guitar and taught himself how to play. After graduating from high school, he got a job as a surveyor, which took him first to Houston and eventually to Nashville, where he played and sang in several informal gospel groups.

In Nashville he met Pappy Daily, an owner of a small local record company. Between 1956 and 1958, LaBeef recorded cover versions of the popular rockabilly hits for Daily's Starday label. Daily played and

sold the disks over local radio. LaBeef moved on to recording for several other small labels throughout the sixties with little success, but he eventually landed a contract with Columbia and recorded his first chart hit, "Every Day," in 1968. However, Columbia dropped him, and the following year he signed with Sam Phillips' Sun Records just before Phillips sold the company to Shelby Singleton. With Singleton, LaBeef recorded his only other single to hit the charts, "Black Land Farmer."

LaBeef is best known for his solid, rockabilly guitar, his basso profundo voice, and his incessant performing. While his music has never been promoted enough to become wildly popular, he still plays energetic and inspired shows to appreciative cult audiences across North America and Europe. His albums include *Bull's Night Out*, *Rockabilly*, *Downhome Rockabilly*, *Western Gold*, *Electricity*, and *It Ain't What You Eat, It's the Way that You Chew It*, the last recorded with D.J. Fontana and Earl Poole, musicians who had played with Elvis Presley and Johnny Cash.

Two rare early photographs of Thomas Paulsley "Sleepy" LaBeef. Sleepy got his nickname while in high school because of his droopy eyelid. When he was fourteen, he traded his rifle for a guitar and taught himself how to play.

The Texas Rockabilly Sound

Like many other rockabilly performers, Roy Orbison started out playing straight country music, with his band the Wink Westerners. When the rockabilly craze hit in 1954 he changed the name of the band to the Teen Kings.

Norman Petty was a Clovis native who moved across the border to Lubbock, Texas, in 1948 to take a job as an assistant recording engineer. While in Lubbock, he played organ in his own band, the Norman Petty Trio, with his wife, Violet Ann, on piano and Jack Vaughn on organ. After playing on the radio and at various clubs around town, Petty moved the band back to Clovis, where he opened his own recording studio in 1954. There the band recorded their one minor hit, a version of the Duke Ellington classic "Mood Indigo." Petty used the money from the record to improve his studio and began recording local rockabilly performers.

A native of Vernon, Texas, Roy Orbison was among the first to record in Petty's studio. Orbison began his musical career while still in high school, with the band Wink Westerners, playing country dance music. With the rise of rockabilly in 1954, Orbison changed

Unlike many other rockabilly stars, Orbison wrote most of his own songs. He was known for his haunting melodies, his high, yodeling voice, and his trademark sunglasses.

the name of the band to the Teen Kings and cut his first record, "Ooby Dooby," in Petty's studio in Clovis. Orbison didn't stay with Petty long; he went to Memphis in 1956 to recut the track as "Oobie Doobie" with Sam Phillips at Sun. The song was credited to Roy Orbison and the Teen Kings, and was a surprise number fifty-nine hit on the pop chart.

Orbison's band split up due to the lack of any follow-up success. He bought his contract back from Phillips, concentrated primarily

Buddy Knox used a cardboard box for percussion on his first hit, "Party Doll," because neither he nor his producer Norman Petty knew how to record rock and roll drums. The two subsequently figured it out and together were responsible for many innovations in the studio.

on songwriting, and scored a hit with "Claudette," which the Everly Brothers put in the top thirty in 1957. Orbison had a few flop rockabilly singles for RCA and Monument before his ballad "Only the Lonely" reached number two in 1959. Orbison rode out the British invasion of the early sixties and recorded twenty top-forty hits between 1959 and 1965, including his only number one hit, "Pretty Woman," in 1964.

Meanwhile, back in Clovis, Norman Petty hooked up with rockabilly innovator Buddy Knox (b. 1933), a guitarist who, with bass player Jimmy Bowen, formed the Rhythm Orchids in 1955. The band cut their first single in Petty's studio in 1956: the A side was "Party Doll," a song written by Knox in 1948; the B side was "I'm Sticking with You," written and sung by Jimmy Bowen. The band used a cardboard box for percussion on both songs because Petty didn't know how to record rock and roll drums. The two songs were released on the local Triple D label and were surprise hits. Roulette, a New York city label, picked up both songs, and released each with its own B side. Each single sold more than one million copies, with "Party Doll" reaching number one and "I'm Sticking with You" going as high as number eleven.

Knox found his true rockabilly style when he added real drums to the band, first with Don Mills and then with former Norman Petty Trio drummer Dave Alldred. Petty quickly learned how to record rock and roll drums, and the Rhythm Orchids were one of the first rockabilly bands to use a trap kit. Knox and Petty grew more adept in the studio and expanded the band to include Bobby Darin on piano, as well as several session musicians in the studio, including Buddy Holly and members of the Crickets.

Between 1957 and 1958, Knox had a total of eight chart-placing singles recorded at Petty's studio and leased to Roulette Records, including "Rock Your Little Baby to Sleep," which hit number seventeen; "Hula Love," a number nine hit; and "Somebody Touched Me," which reached number twenty-two. His last Hot 100 song was "I Think I'm Going to Kill Myself" in 1959, a song that was often banned because of its controversial title.

Knox eventually moved into country pop and had a minor hit as late as 1969 with "Gypsy Man" on UA. While his number of hits equaled that of Buddy Holly's during both of their lifetimes, Knox never gained the popularity or legendary status of his studio mate.

Lubbock, Texas, native Charles Hardin "Buddy" Holly (1936–1959) came from a musical heritage that was hardcore country, but like the other rockabilly performers, he developed an interest in black rhythm and blues by the 1950s. His childhood idol was Hank Williams, but Holly was equally inspired by seeing an early Elvis Presley appearance in Lubbock.

After a few years of playing in clubs, at dances, and on the radio around the Lubbock area, Holly signed with Decca Records at the tender age of nineteen. In 1956, he made three trips to Nashville to work with pioneering country producer Owen Bradley, who produced such landmark artists as Red Foley, Webb Pierce, Ernest Tubb, the Wilburn Brothers, Brenda Lee, Gene Vincent, and Conway Twitty.

Holly's first single was "Blue Days, Black Nights"/ "Love Me." He recorded four more sides with Bradley, including an early version of "That'll Be the Day," but none was successful and Decca dropped him.

Buddy Knox (center) and Jimmy Bowen (top, right) formed the Rhythm Orchids in 1955. Their first single featured a song written and sung by Knox on the A side ("Party Girl") and one written and sung by Bowen on the B side ("I'm Sticking with You").

In 1956, Buddy Holly signed with Decca and recorded four songs in Nashville. However, it was not until he teamed up with producer Norman Petty and musicians Jerry Alison and Sonny Curtis that he hit his true musical stride.

Back in Lubbock, Holly teamed up with drummer Jerry Alison, guitarist Sonny Curtis, bassist Larry Elbron (who was later replaced by Joel B. Maudlin), and pianist Niki Sullivan, and the Crickets went across the border to Norman Petty's studio to record. Holly and Petty became close friends and worked on their recording technique together. Like Buddy Knox, Holly was one of the first rockabilly performers to use a heavy R&B backbeat in his recordings. Petty and Holly were also among the first to experiment with double tracking, overdubbing, and doubling vocals, as on "Words of Love." On "Peggy Sue," Alison played only tom-toms, and Petty recorded with the mike so close to Holly's guitar that a listener can hear the pick scraping across the strings. With Holly's hip, coughing vocal style, the result is an ode to teenage love and angst like nothing ever heard before.

After the band finished recording several songs, Petty offered the tapes to Roulette, who had earlier leased Knox's masters from Petty. Roulette, however, turned Holly down. Petty then sent the tapes to producer Bob Theile, who was running the Coral and Brunswick labels, two divisions of Decca, the company that had dropped Holly a few years earlier. Theile decided to release several songs by the band, some under the name of the Crickets on the Brunswick label, and others under Holly's name on the Coral label.

In 1957, a new version of "That'll Be the Day" by the Crickets went to number one on the pop charts, and the follow-up, "Oh, Boy" (with "Not Fade Away" on the flip side), went to number ten. Later in the same year, Coral released "Peggy Sue"/"Everyday" under Holly's name for a number three hit. In early 1958, the Crickets had two more hits with "Think It Over" and "Rave On," but Holly went to New York to record "Early in the Morning" without the Crickets. Holly's next two songs, "It's So Easy" and "Heartbeat," didn't hit the charts, and by October 1958, Holly had permanently split from both the Crickets and Norman Petty.

Although he was beginning to venture further and further from rockabilly, Holly continued to be an innovator in the studio. One of his last recordings, the Paul Anka song "It Doesn't Matter Anymore," even included strings.

In late 1959, Holly, in desperate need of money, agreed to a lengthy tour with Ritchie Valens and

Norman Petty (left) and Buddy Holly (right) accepting Holly's first gold record for "Peggy Sue."

the Big Bopper (J.P. Richardson). Holly and Valens chartered a plane to get to the next gig in Iowa. At the last minute, Holly's bass player, Waylon Jennings, gave up his seat to the Big Bopper. The plane crashed near Fargo, North Dakota, killing everyone on board. Buddy Holly was only twenty-two.

Rockabilly Madmen

Although his life was tragically cut short, Eddie Cochran proved to be one of the most influential rockabilly artists of all time. He was a polished performer, an innovator in the studio, a capable guitar player, and an excellent songwriter.

With a dark broodiness, voice, a polished, no-holds-barred performance style, and an innate instinct for rock and roll, Eddie Cochran (1938–1960) was one of the most talented rockabilly stars of the 1950s. Like Buddy Holly, Cochran was a perfectionist in the studio, a capable guitar player, and an excellent songwriter. Cochran's greatest strength, however, was in his live performance. He was a dynamic singer who could generate the excitement of Jerry Lee Lewis, while staying polished and in control.

After his family moved to Los Angeles in 1949, Eddie Cochran teamed up with Hank Cochran (no relation) to form his first band. Born Eddie Cochrane, he dropped the "e" from his name so the two could perform as the Cochran Brothers. Hank soon left the band to pursue a career in country music. Eddie, however, was more interested in rockabilly.

Dangerous, sexy, and wild, Gene Vincent and His Blue Caps possessed one of the most dynamic live acts in rock and roll. Their style of gothic rockabilly eventually influenced the psychobilly band The Cramps, among others.

Eddie signed with Liberty in 1957, and his first single was a teen ballad called "Sitting in the Balcony." The song was also a hit on Colonial for Johnny Dee (John D. Loudermilk), who wrote the song. Cochran followed that first record with songs as diverse as "Milk Cow Blues," "Teresa," "Something Else," and "Teenage Heaven." His two best songs were in the classic teen rock genre: "Summertime Blues" is about a kid who can't go out because he has to work late, and "C'mon Everbody" is about another kid who is rolling up the rugs for a party because his parents aren't home.

Cochran's Hollywood home base enabled him to hire some of the best session musicians in the business for his records and also gave him the opportunity to appear in three films: *The Girl Can't Help It* (1956), *Untamed Youth* (1957), and *Go, Johnny, Go* (1958).

In 1959, Cochran recorded a song called "Three Stars" about the deaths of Buddy Holly, the Big Bopper, and Ritchie Valens. This proved to be the ultimate irony, since Cochran's life was also cut short when he died in a car accident in the United Kingdom one year later. Cochran's passenger in the car, fellow rockabilly star Gene Vincent, survived, but was seriously injured.

Vincent Eugene Craddock (1935–1971), was born in Norfolk, Virginia, on February 11, 1935. After the Korean War broke out, Craddock joined the navy and injured his leg badly during combat. The doctors told him it would have to be amputated, but Craddock

Skiffle

Scottish singer Lonnie Donegan was the undisputed king of skiffle, the British answer to rockabilly.

While rockabilly was taking America by storm in the early 1950s, a related form of music was the rage across the Atlantic. Pioneering musicians such as Chris Barber, Ken Coyler, and Lonnie Donegan (b. 1931) were setting the British pop music industry on its ear with a style of music known as "skiffle." Just as rockabilly was a amalgamation of rhythm and blues and hillbilly music, skiffle was a blend of jazz and American folk music.

The word "skiffle" was originally used to describe music played by those too poor to afford musical instruments and who instead used items like washboards, jugs, and washtub basses. The term was borrowed by the British to describe the fast, hillbilly-sounding pop music that inspired the first generation of British rock and rollers.

Scottish singer Lonnie Donegan was the undisputed king of skiffle. His band used a cheap acoustic guitar, a washtub bass, a washboard rhythm section, and very little raw musical talent. The underlying belief behind skiffle was that music was for everyone and that anybody with the desire could form a band—the same belief that has kept rock and roll music alive. Skiffle relied on pumped-up versions of American folk songs by such artists as Leadbelly, Woody Guthrie, and Big Bill Broonzy, as well as country stars such as Hank Williams.

It was the skiffle music of Lonnie Donegan that inspired two young men from Liverpool to pick up their guitars and form their first band, the Quarrymen. Their names were John Lennon and Paul McCartney.

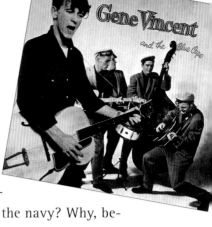

Gene Vincent was an unlikely rock and roll hero. Injured in the Korean war, the gaunt, pale Vincent had to wear a leg brace at all times. Here he is pictured with the Blue Caps on the band's classic second album.

refused to let them. As a result, he had to wear a brace on his leg for the rest of his life. What should a pale, thin, crippled vet do after being discharged from the navy? Why, become a rockabilly star, of course. Craddock came back to the States, changed his name to Gene Vincent, and formed a slick band called the Blue Caps, with Cliff Gallup and Willie Williams on guitars, Jack Neal on bass, and Dickie Harrel on drums.

With the help of a local deejay named Bill "Sheriff Tex" Davis, Vincent wrote his first song, "Be-Bop-A-Lula." The song, based on "Money Honey" and inspired by a Little Lulu comic book, was good enough to get him signed to Capitol Records, a company that were desperate to find an answer to RCA's Elvis Presley.

With gothic, psychopathic vocals and an eerie, driving music track, "Be-Bop-A-Lula" is one of the most overtly sexual rockabilly records of all time. It was the B side of Vincent's "Woman Love," but soon deejays were flipping the single over. The song made it to number seven on the pop charts and number five on the country charts.

Vincent's style was to take Elvis' sexuality and rebel image, along with Buddy Holly's hiccuping vocal style, and increase them tenfold into an orgasmic pant. Dressed in all leather and backed by the ultrahip Blue Caps, Vincent became rockabilly's biggest live draw, although his singles after "Be-Bop-A-Lula" sold poorly due to a lack of promotion (and a refusal to pay payola) on Capitol's part.

While "Race with the Devil" and "Bluejean Bop" may have failed on the radio, they did play on the soundtrack of *The Girl Can't Help It* in 1956. "Lotta Lovin'" hit the chart in 1957, but peaked at number thirteen.

Vincent moved to England in 1959, where he toured hard and drank even harder. In 1960, his leg became reinjured in the car accident that killed Eddie Cochran. His career was never the same; he fell into a lifestyle of womanizing, pill-popping, and heavy drinking. He died in the United Kingdom in 1971 of alcohol-related problems, a bloated parody of his former self.

The Rockabilly Legacy

B y the early 1960s, rockabilly was in serious trouble. Elvis had gone into the army and was later trapped in a musically stifling film career; Jerry Lee Lewis was caught up in scandal; Buddy Holly had been killed in a plane crash; and car accidents had stalled the careers of Carl Perkins and Gene Vincent. Johnny Horton, a country singer who was married to Hank Williams' widow, was set to burst onto the rockabilly scene when a car crash sent him to sudden infamy in 1960.

Even outside rockabilly, rock and roll music was in trouble. Chuck Berry was arrested for taking an underage woman across state lines, and Little Richard had given up rock and roll for God. The best of black rock and roll was once again being sanitized, watered-down, and repackaged into hits for "safe" white acts such as Fabian and Paul Anka.

The Everly Brothers epitomized the later, softer side of rockabilly. Don and Phil Everly enjoyed a long career that was unfortunately marred by an infamous sibling rivalry.

The day the music died: The wreckage of the single engine Bonanza that went down soon after takeoff, killing Buddy Holly, Ritchie Valens, J.P. "The Big Bopper" Richardson, and pilot Roger Peterson.

Even the rockabilly legends who did survive the early sixties, such as Roy Orbison, the Everly Brothers, Brenda Lee, Wanda Jackson, Ronnie Hawkins, Johnny and Dorsey Burnette, and Charlie Feathers, moved either into country music or into instant obscurity. While rockabilly was never the same after 1960, it did provide inspiration for the bands that would take rock and roll into the next three decades. Ubiquitous bands of the sixties, such as the Beatles (whose name was inspired by the Crickets), the Rolling Stones, the

Brian Setzer of the Stray Cats, a rockabilly revival band that sprang out of the New Wave music movement of the 1980s.

The Clash (left to right: Joe Strummer, Mick Jones, Paul Simonon, and Topper Headon) borrowed the Crickets' "I Fought the Law" as well as rockabilly's rebellious attitude.

Yardbirds, the Faces, and many more, have cited the likes of Buddy Holly, Eddie Cochran, Carl Perkins, Roy Orbison, and Elvis Presley as inspiration for their music, and have recorded cover versions of rockabilly songs both famous and obscure.

In the 1970s, when the punk rock movement tried to make rock and roll both fun and dangerous again, many of the hits and sounds that originally gave rock and roll its vitality were revived. Elvis Costello took the King's name and fashioned himself into a demented version of Buddy Holly. The Sex Pistols' Sid Vicious recorded versions of "C'mon Everybody" and "Something Else" that would have made Eddie Cochran proud. The Clash borrowed the Crickets' "I Fought the Law." And the Ramones took the basic one-three-five musical form of rockabilly and turned it into anthems of 1970s urban teenage angst.

In 1979, guitarist Brain Setzer (b. 1959), bassist Lee Rocker (born Lee Drucher, 1961), and drummer Slim Jim Phantom (born James McDonell, 1961) formed a rockabilly revival trio called the Stray Cats. They specialized in authentic-sounding rockabilly with a new-wave edge, complete with stand-up bass, hollow-body guitar, and a trimmed-down drum kit. Produced by fellow rockabilly lover Dave Edmunds, the Stray Cats scored a series of hits in the early eighties, including "Stray Cat Strut," "Runaway Boys," and "Rock This Town." While the band broke up after their second album failed, Setzer later appeared with George Harrison on a television tribute to Carl Perkins in 1986.

Conclusion

From the gritty lyrics and honky tonk sounds of Hank Williams, the jazz-influenced country swing of Bob Wills, and the hillbilly yodelings of Riley Puckett and Red Foley to the country blues of Blind Lemon Jefferson, the jump sounds of Louis Jordan, and the high-energy rock and roll of Chuck Berry and Little Richard, country music and rhythm and blues have always shared a similar spirit, energy, and inventiveness. Both forms of music were looked down upon by the increasingly homogenous middle class of the 1940s and 1950s. Prior to 1949, rhythm and blues was listed as "race" music on the *Billboard* charts, and country music was listed as "hillbilly" music. Both music styles had their roots in the music of southern rural America—blues, gospel, and folk—and both were developed by the poorer segments of American society. It was inevitable that the two forms of music would eventually collide.

In the early 1950s, Fats Domino, Chuck Berry, Little Richard, the Dominoes, and countless other black musicians were well on their way to turning rhythm and blues into rock and roll. Theirs was a new, up-tempo, exciting form of music that white America was slow to catch on to. While white teenagers clandestinely listened to black radio and record companies experimented with toned-down cover versions of R&B hits, a group of wild, young white musicians across the south started playing rhythm and blues the only way they knew how—with a hillbilly twist.

Carl Perkins, shown here in a still for *Jamboree*, performed "Glad All Over" in the movie.

Rockabilly legends such as Elvis Presley, Buddy Holly, Eddie Cochran, Carl Perkins, and Jerry Lee Lewis were able to bring rock and roll to the forefront of the American music scene. They helped break the race barrier in rock and roll, and they brought their loud, hard-driving, in-your-face style of music directly into the American living room. While the heyday of rockabilly lasted only a few years— roughly from 1954 to 1960—and most of its chief practitioners were burnt out, copped out, or were killed, its importance in the history of American music cannot be overlooked.

The rockabilly performers were the first rock and roll rebels who helped pioneer the musical form that has dominated popular culture for the past forty years. They borrowed from all of the music they loved—country, gospel, rhythm and blues—melded the sounds together, and played the only way they knew how—fast and furious. Rockabilly was music for the young and wild, and it sang to hearts and minds of all teenagers who were tired of listening to their parents and who yearned for something vital and exciting in their lives. It is in this spirit that rock and roll has survived since its inception.

Suggested Listening

Suggested Listening

Suggested Listening

Cochran, Eddie. *Singin' to My Baby/ Never to Be.* (Capitol)

Haley, Bill, and His Comets. *From the Original Master Tapes.* (UNI/MCA)

Holly, Buddy. *Chirping Crickets.* (UNI/MCA)

——. *The Complete Buddy Holly.* (UNI/MCA)

Jackson, Wanda. *Rockin' in the Country.* (Rhino)

Knox, Buddy. *The Best of Buddy Knox.* (Rhino)

LaBeef, Sleepy. *Human Jukebox.* (Sun Entertainment)

——. *Strange Things Happen.* (Rounder Records)

Lee, Brenda. *Anthology, 1956–1980.* (UNI/MCA)

Lewis, Jerry Lee. *All Killer, No Filler: Anthology.* (Rhino)

——. *Classic.* (Bear Family)

Perkins, Carl. *Classics.* (Bear Family)

——. *Original Sun Greatest Hits.* (Rhino)

Presley, Elvis. *The Million Dollar Quartet.* (RCA)

——. *The Sun Sessions.* (RCA)

Stray Cats. *Best of Stray Cats: Rock This Town.* (Capitol)

Various. *Memphis Rocks: Rockabilly in Memphis, 1954-1968.* (Smithsonian)

Various. *Rockabilly Shakeout.* (Ace [U.K.])

Various. *Rock the Town: Rockabilly Hits Vols. 1 and 2.* (Rhino)

Vincent, Gene. *Gene Vincent: Capitol Collectors Series.* (Capitol)

——. *Greatest Hits.* (Atlantic)

Suggested Reading

Amburn, Ellis. *Dark Star: The Roy Orbison Story.* New York: Lyle Stuart, 1992.

Clarke, Donald, ed. *The Penguin Encyclopedia of Popular Music.* New York: Viking/Penguin, 1989.

Clarke, Donald. *The Rise and Fall of Popular Music.* New York: St. Martin's Press, 1995.

Decurtis, Anthony, James Henke, Holly George-Warren, and Jim Miller, eds. *The Rolling Stone Illustrated History of Rock and Roll: The Definitive History of the Most Important Artists & Their Music.* New York: Random House, 1992.

Du Noyer, Paul. S. *The Story of Rock 'n' Roll.* New York: Macmillan, 1995.

Ellis, Amburn. *Buddy Holly: A Biography.* New York: St. Martin's Press, 1995.

Escott, Colin, and Martin Hawkins. *Good Rockin' Tonight: Sun Records and the Birth of Rock and Roll.* New York: St. Martin's Press, 1992.

Fornatale, Pete. *The Story of Rock 'n' Roll.* New York: William Morrow and Company, 1987.

Frew, Tim. *Elvis: His Life and Music.* New York: Friedman/Fairfax, 1994.

Jackson, John A. *Big Beat Heat: Alan Freed and the Early Years of Rock 'n' Roll.* New York: Macmillan, 1995.

Marcus, Greil, *Mystery Train.* New York: Dutton, 1975.

Marsh, Dave. *Elvis.* New York: Rolling Stone Press, 1982.

Palmer, Robert. *Rock and Roll: An Unruly History.* New York: Harmony, 1995.

Romanowski, Patricia, ed. *New Rolling Stone Encyclopedia of Rock and Roll.* New York: Fireside, 1995.

Szatmary, David P. *Rockin' in Time: A Social History of Rock and Roll.* New York: Prentice Hall, 1995.

Tosches, Nick. *Unsung Heroes of Rock 'n' Roll.* New York: Harmony, 1991.

Various. *The History of Rock—Birth of Rock 'n' Roll.* New York: Hal Leonard Publishing Corp, 1990.

Index

Photo credits